14 Days With God

Dr. Gwendolyn Matthews

Unless otherwise indicated, all Scripture quotations are from the

New King James Version

New International Version

Fourteen Days with God

All Rights Reserved

Softcover Edition

eBook ISBN: 9780578731414

Book ISBN: 978-0-578-73139-1

Printed in the United States of America

2012 by Dr. Gwendolyn Matthews

Affordable Publishing & Print

San Diego, California

The Library of Congress has cataloged the

trade paperback edition as follows:

14 Days with God by Dr. Gwendolyn Matthews

No part of this book may be reproduced or transmitted in any form or by any means, electronic or mechanical, including photocopy, recording, or by any information storage and retrieval system, without permission in writing from the publisher.

Copyright © 2012

Table of Contents

Day 1 1

Day 2 19

Day 3 39

Day 4 49

Day 5 56

Day 6 63

Day 7 75

Day 8 84

Day 9 90

Day 10 101

Day 11 108

Day 12 112

Day 13 122

Day 14 129

Dedication

I dedicate this book to the love of my life, Jesus Christ.

Day 1

Yesterday as I woke up to prepare for yet another ministry engagement, not having much strength, I felt fragile and had an excruciating headache. I dragged myself out of bed as if I needed the assistance of a crane to pull these hips upward to hoist my body out of bed.

When I got to my feet, I stumbled a bit and thought, "I have to press through this last engagement before I can rest!" I found it difficult to put my clothes on. I kept experiencing shortness of breath like someone with emphysema. I called my assistant and told her to bring me some orange juice and a bottle of Dayquil to give me energy and soothe my aching body. I brushed it off and thought it was a cold or the flu.

When I looked outside, it was pouring down rain, and I could feel the cold chill coming from the crack in the window. I grabbed a jacket, and as I heard the doorbell ring, my assistant came in and said in a concerned voice, "You look horrible. Are you all right?" I told her I felt terrible, but I knew under the anointing of God, my achiness would go away, as it always does when I am not feeling my best. The anointing is so incredible! It is as if God takes you out of your strength and infuses you with His supernatural strength and power that can only come from Him.

I prayed before I ministered to the Word and asked the Lord to strengthen me and allow His Spirit to minister to his people. God answered my prayer, as He always does. As the Word of God came forth, with power and truth, the Holy Spirit flooded the atmosphere. The people praised the Lord and received the gift of encouragement and the hope that God would be with them during their times of struggle.

It never ceases to amaze me that while under the influence of the Holy Spirit, I had no pain, no coughing, no sneezing, and not one symptom appeared. I felt larger-than-life. After ministering the Word, I stood at the altar, laying hands on the people and, the prophetic gift was operating flawlessly. As I prayed for the last person, the Holy Spirit revealed the person's life as a movie on a big screen, and we were all amazed as the details unfolded. You would have thought I knew that person all her life, but I had only met her that day.

I took my seat and noticed my clothes were drenched wet from the perspiration secreted from my sweat glands and onto my body. As I sat waiting for the benediction, I felt all my strength leave my body, my head began to ache, and I almost fell over from exhaustion. One thing for sure, I was feeling sick again. It became alarmingly clear that something was wrong, and I needed to see a doctor. Immediately after service, my assistant and I, along with my mother, headed straight to urgent care.

The doctor saw me right away and ran a series of tests. He left and then returned to the examining room and said, "Gwen, you have walking pneumonia." I have walking pneumonia! I can't believe it! I've never had pneumonia, so I couldn't believe what I was hearing. I have always been healthy except for a minor cold or the flu.

When the doctor informed me that I had pneumonia, the first thing he told me was, "You must slow down." I then asked, "How many days?" Before he could open his mouth, my mother interjected, "She needs at least two weeks!" She told him, "She is a Pastor, and she is always busy. Gwen travels here and there, speaking and teaching in different cities and states." My Mom went on to say, "When Gwen is in town, she provides support and counseling to all those in need, making sure everyone is okay while also managing the church. So, as you can imagine, she's pulled here and there with no time for herself, and it has become her way of life." My Mom was unrelenting and made sure to reiterate my need for two weeks of rest.

I want to share something with you briefly about my mother, my dear sweet mother. She is an amazing lady. All my life, she has taken care of our family, two boys and two girls. Not only has she taken care of us, but she has also taken care of everyone in our neighborhood from as far back as I can remember. Growing up, I don't think my friends even knew her real name — everyone just called her "Mom."

Without hesitation, my doctor agreed with my mother and instructed me to stay in for the full two weeks. Laughing to myself, "He must be a "Mama's boy!" My doctor prescribed antibiotics to treat pneumonia and acetaminophen for the pain. He gave strict instructions for bed rest and to stay in the house for at least two weeks. Fourteen days would be a long time for me. I had to get better soon! There must be some fast-track step-by-step plan I can follow or some super medicine that can heal me quickly, preferably right now because I can't stand to be in one place, especially for that long.

While I was in the doctors' office, I felt an unction in my spirit to ask my doctor about meditation. I asked him what the benefits of meditation are? He began to explain that it is good for the mind and the body. When the mind is not at rest, it does not send the proper signals to the body to rest and heal itself. There is spiritual significance to that statement.

My doctor asked me if I was going to start meditation? I told him, "No, I'm going to start praying. For the Believer, praying is a form of meditation." He looked at me and smiled, and walked out of the examining room.

  I left the doctor's office and headed straight to the pharmacy to get my prescription filled. As we sat waiting in the pharmacy, I thought to myself, "What was I going to do in the house for fourteen days?" Hello! I have never been anywhere for that length of time, not even my own home. I thought to myself, "I am going to pray until I get well. I'll quote Scriptures and take all my medicine. It can't be too bad. There are only seven pills to take. I'll take one pill today. Then, I will only have to stay in the house for six more days. By Sunday, it will all be over! Yeah, that's what I'll do,"… so, I thought.

  I realized this would be the start of a new journey. For me, this journey was my time to bring forth revelation to my mind and rest for my body. I realized that the time I would spend sitting in silence and solitude recovering would be the much-needed time I would spend with God. I stopped fussing and complaining about having to stay in the house because I realized that the Holy Spirit was calling me to Himself for the next fourteen days.

As usual, my husband, Charlie, was there waiting for my arrival. I explained what happened and the instructions the doctor gave me. My husband is a strong-willed man, and I could hear the firmness in his voice. "Gwen, the doctor, said fourteen days in the house, and you will be in for fourteen days." Just by his tone, I knew there was no way of getting around it. There's no sense in me trying to negotiate with Mr. Charles Matthews!

Immediately, he sent out an email notifying the leaders in our church to contact their teams to inform them that I would be quarantined and on bed rest for fourteen days. He instructed them not to disturb me. That means no emails, no Facebook, no phone calls, no text, and no one to drop by the house. I needed to get rest. I thought to myself, "You must be kidding me. No contact with the outside world?" I felt like I was in prison. I'm isolated from the world! I know he loves me and wants me to get well, but I felt like this was too extreme, and it was going to drive me crazy. My assistant was on the same page as my husband. The two of them were determined to make sure I rested and followed the doctors' orders.

    My first day began quiet and peaceful. My assistant came over early that next morning. She gave me my medicine, made me hot cups of tea, and made sure I was eating. She also purchased a blood pressure monitor to take my blood pressure every day. She was amazing! She kept me on a strict regimen. I don't know what I would have done without her. I began to call her "*The Warden*"... isn't that funny?

    In my restless state, I called an old friend, who I knew would understand and appreciate my journey. We talked a lot about the church, where we are as a body in Christ, leadership, and the state of the world. Our conversation got to a point where I began to get so worked up that I almost couldn't catch my breath. My Assistant could hear the change in my breathing as I spoke, and she quickly came over to me and checked my blood pressure. Sure enough, it was high. All the while, I kept hearing in my spirit, "Rest, Gwen, rest!"

In my pursuit of rest and recovery, I was still restless. I decided to cook dinner. Isn't that hilarious? Surely, God wouldn't be upset with me for cooking dinner for my family, would He? Cooking sounded good to me. Besides, I love to cook. Cooking relaxes me. What better way to relax! So, I convinced myself that God gave me His approval and started planning my meal. My menu consisted of slow-roasted Cornish Game Hens in a rosemary herb sauce with seasoned red potatoes and cheesy garlic vegetables. You must admit, that sounds glorious. I thought to myself what a great wife and mother I am, and yet again, I heard, "Rest Gwen, rest!"

I decided to dismiss what I heard, and I continued buzzing around the kitchen. Around 6 o'clock, everything shifted, and oh my goodness, what a drastic shift! I became overtaken by exhaustion. I felt every ounce of strength in my body leave me like a crowd of people scattering off in different directions at the sound of a gunshot in a public place. My breathing became shallow again. My head started pounding. I felt like I was right back where I started. I needed to lie down. When I said I needed to lie down, I meant right at that moment, or I would pass out! My assistant could see I was having a problem and that I was not well. She guided me back upstairs to lay down so that my head would stop spinning.

While lying down, I thought it was a great idea to get up and cook for my family, but clearly, it wasn't. I also realized; I was struggling to be still. Do you want to know what else God revealed to me? He said that I can't get rid of pneumonia in one day, not even if I am anointed. Can I get an amen?

I never thought it would take so much effort to be still. Being still was a full-fledged war within itself. For me to sit on the couch and do absolutely nothing, that's just not me. I realized that I have been running for so long, expanding myself non-stop, which created a living pattern that caused my mind and body to function on autopilot. I was moving without any conscious consideration of how I was pushing my body to unhealthy limits. That was how I landed where I was. Every effort to be still was a challenge. I would sit down for one minute only to jump up the next minute to figure out something to do. Help me, Lord!

I felt as though I needed a Spiritual straitjacket to force me into stillness. It became apparent that being still was too daunting for me. I let my thoughts wander too much. Sometimes I allowed glamorous, imaginative, self-seeking, and glory-driven thoughts about what I was going to receive at the end of the fourteen days to plague my mind. I grabbed hold of my mind, and I repented. Was I going to be more powerful, more anointed, and more discerning? Why does everything have to be about me? Why do I have to be glorified?

I asked the Father, "Are the thoughts of wanting to be glorified a satanic stream that flows through me?" "Or is it the fact that we are your children, and we love being in your glory, so much so that we seek to be there subconsciously?" The Spirit of God answered me with this, "finding glory through the flesh can never be my will for your life!"

In moments of rest, I began thinking about my prayer life. There were questions I needed to ask God and myself:
1. "God, do I run into your presence to dump off my requested mail?
2. You know my list of needs and the needs of others?
3. Father, do I take the time to listen for an answer when I pray?
4. When was the last time I sat with You just because I love You?"

I knew the answers, but I struggled to confess the answers aloud. It had been too long!

I continued to pray, "Father, if this is the revelation that you're giving me, do I run myself down with the cares and duties of life and ministry?" I believe the enemy knows that those who genuinely love God and want to do His will, will never abandon their purpose and destiny and never cease to give selflessly to help people in need. For those who are like me, who will never walk away from the call, the enemy will try to kill us on the job.

Oh, how we need the Lord's wisdom with us always to lead and guide us into all truths so that we don't allow our ignorance to destroy us. I began to pray, "Father, discipline my body, and help me learn how to sit in your presence, and while I am there, teach me how to stay in each moment with you. Father, help me learn how to listen to your voice like I used to. The voice that brought me to you, the voice that taught me, and the voice that loves me." I get it now.

God is so wise. He arrests our lives in ways that we can't even imagine. I believe not only was the Lord calling me to rest, but He was also calling me to Himself. Do you know that God wants to be with you more than you can imagine? My whole attitude about staying in the house changed instantly. Now I am excited about this fourteen-day journey.

Journal Your Thoughts

Why is it so difficult to be still in the presence of the LORD?

_____
_____
_____
_____
_____
_____
_____
_____
_____
_____
_____
_____
_____
_____
_____
_____
_____
_____
_____
_____
_____
_____
_____
_____

My Prayer

"Father, I pray that being in your presence will never be a chore! Your presence has always been my place of refuge and strength. Being in your presence was never motivated by what I needed but was motivated by my love for being with you. Father, I remember praying if my title or position would ever get in the way of our relationship, then take it back! Father, I made myself sick, but I thank you for this time of rest. I understand that the most important place to be in this world or the world to come is in your presence. In Jesus' Name, Amen."

Take a Moment

Reflect on your time with the Lord. Are you just dropping off mail requests, or are you spending quality time with the Him? What are you allowing to get in the way of your time with Jesus? Journal your thoughts.

Day 2

I woke up around 3 a.m. How can you begin your day at 3 a.m.? 3 a.m. is when I got up to pray. I made my way upstairs trying to walk silently like a mom trying not to wake her children. When I got to my couch, I laid my head on the soft cushion. I felt the presence of the Lord there, right where I laid my head, and I rested in prayer. My whole being exhaled. My mind, my emotions, and my will surrendered to His presence, and I rested!

One of the places I meet Jesus is on my couch upstairs by the window. When I need to get alone time with the Lord, that's one of my many places I would go. He's always there waiting for me. I go there and sit quietly until I feel His peace in and around me.

I want to ask you a question.

Where is your resting place with Jesus? Where is that place where you can go and be still? Where is the place that you can go and know He will always be there waiting for you?

One of the other places I go to meet Him is at Sunset Cliffs in San Diego. There I'd sit at the edge of the cliff overlooking the sea. I would sit and contemplate how powerful He is.

When my life is so bogged down or overwhelmed with the cares of the world I will go, sit, and think in that place. One particular day I remember marveling at the thought, "If the Lord can command the sea to roll in and roll out again without overtaking the shore, surely, He can take care of my issues."

I found another beautiful spot at the La Jolla Shores, where I walk down off the cliffs through the apertures to a site where the Spirit led me. In that location, facing the beauty of the waves and the rocks surrounding me, I thought of the deep waters that reminded me of the depth of His love for me. The water crashed against the rocks; the spray of the sea caressed my face; it was as if the Lord had kissed me on my cheeks
I looked down into the depth of the sea, trying to see the bottom, but never saw it. It reminds

me of God's eternal love for me. I will never understand how deep His love flows for me in this lifetime, yet somehow, I know.

Another spot where Jesus and I would meet was in my backyard. I have a huge grapefruit tree that yields fruit all year round. The fragrance of the budding flowers is intoxicating. There in my backyard, I have a view overlooking the city.

I used to frequent that place more because it is so peaceful. I don't know why I don't visit it as much, but when I do, there is a sweet peace waiting for me and a welcoming presence that comes in the form of a breeze embracing my body and elevating my mind. In this spiritual place most familiar to me, I am in a higher realm, a peaceful and holy place. There, I find Jesus. These are just a few of the places we would meet: my lover and me, my sweet Jesus.

Reflection

What are the words of affection that you whisper to the Father in your meeting place? If you don't have a love language, begin to speak well of Him and speak words of love and affection to the lover of your soul. Some of my words of affection are Abba, Father, Holy One.

_____
_____
_____
_____
_____
_____
_____
_____
_____
_____
_____
_____
_____
_____
_____
_____
_____
_____

Let me get back to my 3 a.m. encounter. As I became familiar with this place of rest, abruptly, my spirit became disturbed and uneasy. Fearful thoughts came like a flood and invaded my peace. Wait one minute! I thought this was going to be a place of rest. What was happening with these anxious thoughts? As soon as my consciousness met my subconscious, the war began.

Often, when you relax, unresolved issues will arise in your subconscious and begin to plague your mind and overtake your thoughts. Thoughts of loss, thoughts of loneliness, insecurities, and fear. You see, there are dark forces that come to steal, kill, and destroy, even your peace. I couldn't keep still. There was a battle happening in my mind, and I struggled to stay in God's presence. Even amid this mental battle, I heard my Savior saying, "Rest in my lap, Gwen."

I tried to regain focus and relax, but thoughts of death showed up, and for whatever reason, all I could think about was my children. I went into a panic in my soul, and I began to war for their lives. I started praying for each one of them. While still frantic, I grabbed my iPad and stalked my children's Facebook pages to check on their last posts. I sent each one of my children a prayer. I typed out the most beautiful prayers and thought, "Whew, my children are safe!" Although I verbalized that they were safe, I didn't feel it in my heart until I heard the Lord say, "Rest here in my lap."

After hearing the Lord say, "Rest Gwen," I knew in my spirit that my children were safe. I tried to relax yet again, but this time the attack came towards me. The negative thoughts penetrated my mind, yet again, and told me to say goodbye to my children and husband. Sometimes, we forget that there are dark forces in the world that infuse negative thoughts in our minds. We often think those thoughts are ours, not knowing that they are implanted into our minds in hopes that we will act on them. The playground for the dark forces is your thought life. If those forces can get you to believe that those negative thoughts are yours, even though they are not, those forces take control of your peace, leading to control of your life.

Imagine how many people believe these thoughts. The bible says to cast down every imagination and every vain thing that exalts itself against the knowledge of God and to bring into captivity every thought to the obedience of Christ. Those forces said that the church would be okay without me. These thoughts bombarded my mind like a cavalry of soldiers charging into an intense battle. I wondered, "Is this why I am in the house? Is it time for me to die, Father? An overwhelming sadness came upon me, and I thought, I am not finished with my work yet. I thought to myself, "I have so much more to do."

All these questions started plaguing my mind, and I had a thousand more questions frantically running around in my head like an anthill disturbed by a spray of Raid. "Rest, Gwen" I heard the Lord say in a strong, confident, yet soothing voice. So, I brought those negative and dark thoughts into submission, spoke the word of God over my life, and came back to that place of peace. If you can control your thoughts you can control your emotions, when you control your emotions, you control your actions.

I took a deep breath and focused my ears on the gentle whisper of a loving Savior, and the sound of the dark thoughts became dim and disappeared as if it was snuffed out like a lit cigarette! – pss. What a Savior! When we focus on Jesus, He will silence the voice of the enemy just like that!

The Lord said the enemy is trying to make you believe that you are dying before your time and that your children are dying soon, but the truth is, no one is going anywhere for a long time. So, rest! The Lord said, "While you are resting, I am going to heal your body." The Lord instructed me to speak peace over my mind, and I obeyed. Immediately peace entered my spirit like the sun breaking through rain clouds, and I exhaled in my spirit and soul. Peace came over me like a warm blanket on a baby at bedtime with loving parents nearby singing a precious lullaby as the child drifts off into a confident sleep. Finally, the rest came.

Record What Happens

Take some time and sit quietly. Are there negative thoughts in your mind? Speak peace over yourself and ask the Lord to sit with you. Ask Him to allow you to experience His presence right now. Be still. Don't get anxious. Exhale and wait. Write about your experience.

_____
_____
_____
_____
_____
_____
_____
_____
_____
_____
_____
_____
_____
_____
_____
_____

I can't tell you exactly what time it was. Maybe around 9 a.m. when my rest was interrupted by the sound of the doorbell. My assistant was at the door. It is time to get up. I answered the door and welcomed her gentle smile into my home. She was faithful to fulfill her assignment of guarding the front door and my cell phone.

My dwelling place for this day was my family room. I turned on the television to watch TBN, a Christian television station. This particular day had a great lineup! Everything was feeding my spirit; the worship was beautiful. The Word was excellent. I cannot remember the last time I sat and watched TBN uninterrupted. My soul was being fed, and I was feeling life being poured back into my spirit. Everything is great after you've been in the presence of Jesus. It was around noon when I began to feel a little fatigued. So, I closed my eyes to take a nap, something that I seldom do. I dreamt many dreams while I slept, but I can't remember any of them. One thing I did remember, though, they were peaceful.

As I woke from my nap, I thought, more TBN and more worship! I spent the rest of the day watching different programs on TBN. I forgot how much I enjoyed watching the worship programs. This ended up being a great day. Although it had its fair share of challenges as I worked through some mental battles, I felt strength infusing my body and spirit as I continued to rest. It's interesting how know what to do, know when to do it, know exactly where to do it, and we even understand why we should rest, but we don't do it. We don't spend enough time relaxing in the presence of the Lord. What are we so afraid of?

My Prayer

Father, on this journey, let us desire Your presence more than anything. I want us to delight in Your presence. Let us not fear Your presence. Our time with You is so precious. As my body mends, help me prioritize my life to maximize the time spent with You. I know that in Your presence, there is a fullness of joy that I so desire. I love you, Abba. Abba, help us to remember that every negative thought is not ours. Please help us to replace negative thoughts with positive thoughts.

Journal Your Thoughts

What is the enemy using to plague your mind? What lies is he telling you that are keeping you from living your life to its fullness?

_____
_____
_____
_____
_____
_____
_____
_____
_____
_____
_____
_____
_____
_____
_____
_____
_____
_____
_____
_____
_____
_____

Now, replace those negative thoughts with positive affirmations.

_____
_____
_____
_____
_____
_____
_____
_____
_____
_____
_____
_____
_____
_____
_____
_____
_____
_____
_____
_____
_____
_____
_____
_____
_____
_____
_____
_____

Doesn't that feel better?

Day 3

Today, I decided to stay in bed, and I found myself falling in and out of sleep. I began to dream about my mentor Dr. Lauretta Gonzalez, who has gone home to be with the Lord. In the dream, Dr. Gonzalez and I were in a helicopter. I was telling her about all the things we had experienced by the power of God. She was fussing about being in a helicopter and said we were moving too fast. I told her to relax and enjoy the ride.

As we flew over the ocean, it looked so vast and appeared to be boundless, filled with different shades of blue and green. As the helicopter glided over the sea, I could see that we were moving fast. It was as though we were on a roller coaster. I felt great exhilaration and excitement as we moved up, down, and around. Our bodies would lean to the left, lean to the right, and then forward, being held in place by our seatbelts. You could feel every jolt so vividly.

I was showing her all the ground that we had covered in that helicopter. As we descended close to the water, I remember a chasm between one ocean and the other. I remember thinking to myself, "There were two continents divided, and the ravine was as deep as the Grand Canyon."

The one ocean that we visited was arrayed in baby blue, and the waves were dancing on the ocean. It was about midday, and the sun was out. The helicopter began to rise in the heavens, and while we were ascending higher and higher, we were able to see how broad one side of the ocean was compared to the other. Our eyes were fixed on the horizon. The beauty was overwhelming. The rays of sunlight were kissing the ocean like a young couple in love, and with a delightful response, the waves reached up to embrace the sunlight. It was just gorgeous. The helicopter began to lean to the right, descending closer to the ocean. We were driving very fast and at an angle that I had never been in before. However, I was not afraid. I knew that the pilot had complete control of the vessel, and whatever maneuvers the pilot made, I was in perfect sync with Him. That pilot was Jesus.

We got to the chasm in the ocean. Although there was no break in the water, I could not see where the water started or where it ended. It was sort of like Niagara Falls. The water covered both continents. As I got to the other continent, the sun began to set, and the sky that was once baby blue turned to royal and navy blue. In the midst of all that blue, I saw what seemed like glitter. Yes! Gold glitter sparkling in between the shades of blue. I believe it was dusk at that time. The rhapsody of colors made me think of Las Vegas at night. If you've ever been to Las Vegas at night, it's something to behold. At night in Las Vegas, the lights illuminate the sky, and it feels as if you are on another planet. At night, the city comes alive with thrilling excitement. The energy is insane, and that is how I felt when I was looking at this particular continent.

You're probably wondering why I am sharing this dream with you. The dream's significance is not what I dreamt, although I know what it meant for me. It was the fact that after resting, I started dreaming again! I had not dreamt like that in a long time. So vivid, so clear. I used to dream all of the time. Dreaming for me was one of the ways God would communicate with me. Now that I think about it, I became too busy to realize that I was not dreaming as frequently as I once did and that my dreams were different when I did dream. My dreams were darker than usual. I didn't feel as connected to God as I usually did.

Day three was the beginning of many revelations. The first revelation is that the more time you spend with God, the more God reveals to you. The second is that the more I began drifting from God, the darker demonic forces could plague our minds.

Being at the feet of Jesus and resting in Him will unlock your dream gates. It is amazing how God can speak to you in dreams. The first continent in the dream was where the ministry is, and though it is in a good place, it can't compare with where it is going, as seen in the second continent. God wants to talk to you in your dreams. Are you dreaming?

Journal Your Thoughts

When you rest in Jesus, not only does your body get rest, but your mind and spirit get rest also. The Holy Spirit in you can hear from Heaven in a dream and share the secrets and the mysteries of God in your subconscious. Jesus can use any avenue He chooses to get messages to us, even in our dreams.

How are you dreaming? What are you dreaming of? Is your mind so cluttered that when you go to sleep, you pass out? Is your mind so cluttered with the things of the world that when you dream, you are only dreaming about what you must do tomorrow? Are you trying to process what you didn't have time to process from the day before? Has your dream life been interrupted by you being busy?

_____

_____
_____
_____
_____
_____
_____

As You Are Journaling Today

Write down some of the dreams that you remember having lately. Put a date on it and then start spending more time with the Lord and see how your dreams change.

Day 4

Day four was unexpectedly busy. I had a couple of people stop by to check in on me. The only reason why they got in the house was that my assistant, "the warden," was not there to keep them out. The first person that came by to visit me was one of my godsons. I always enjoy talking with him because we would always talk about the Lord. He is very gifted young man. I believe as he yields to the leading of the Holy Spirit, and as he allows the Holy Spirit to break him and temper him, he will be a mighty prophet one day.

The second visitor I had, I will call him Thomas. Thomas is like a brother to me, and my heart aches for him. I love him dearly, but he is broken and is still battling the trauma of an abusive childhood. As usual ,the conversation turned toward him and all the women in his life. We've been friends for a long time, and our conversations seldom rise past the flesh. I long for the day when the abundance out of his mouth will be more about God than about women. I know that

God has an amazing call on his life, but I also know that the only way he will fulfill that call is to walk through the process of healing. My friend needs healing in his soul, and I know that God wants to do it. Thomas also must choose to truly live for Jesus.

Many people in this world have not had the love, affirmation, acceptance, and nurturing they deserved when brought into this world, which could be because their parents were broken vessels. After delivering a child, the mother and the father's job is to speak empowering affirmations to their children, making them believe that there is nothing they cannot achieve. When parents don't give their children the love, acceptance, and affirmation they need to become a whole person, they spend the rest of their lives similar to Thomas, seeking their identity, purpose, and place in the world, and that could be a sorrowful life.

Love, affirmations, acceptance, and nurturing are things we should have gotten in our formative years, but if we didn't, they can still be found in a relationship with Jesus

Christ and his word. I know for sure that these things can be found in Jesus because I sought a relationship with him, and he fulfilled all of those things in me.

I was the product of a broken home. My father could have been the author of the song "Papa was a Rolling Stone." I would hear from my father every seven years, and when I did, he was always intoxicated. My father's absence allowed a spirit of abandonment and rejection to enter into my life. A father's role is to help you feel secure in love and protected, and when he didn't fulfill that role, those dark spirits began to bring counterfeits in the form of broken male relationships. I could not trust them because I could not trust my father. If I did get into a healthy relationship, I would sabotage it out of fear that they would reject and abandon me as my father did, and I did not want to feel that pain again.

My mother, bless her heart, was a single parent working two jobs to ensure that her four children had food to eat and clothes to wear. One thing my mother always did was foster a strong relationship between Jesus and all of her children. My brothers and sister would lay in the bed with my mom at night, and she would sing the Lord's prayer to us and pray with us. She would always tell us how much Jesus loved us and that he would always take care of us. Thomas did not have that experience. He is still searching for what can only be found in Jesus.

Thomas sat as long as he did, which was about 35 minutes, because "The Warden" had not arrived yet. When she arrived, she came directly into the den and said to Thomas, "I hope you're not pulling on her or dumping on her because she needs to get her rest!" The tone of her voice was forthright and serious. She checked my blood pressure, which, of course, was high again, and told me, "You got to stop, Pastor. You have to rest!" This time she warned me and told me that God is not playing with me. I felt like a five-year-old being scolded by a favorite aunt. I agreed with her and apologized. I cut my conversation with Thomas short. He apologized for dumping and left. I was drained by the negative energy of the conversation. I decided to listen to the

Word of God and not allow any more visitors.

When you sit with friends or family, and the conversation is draining and negative, it affects your spirit and can disturb your peace. I needed to get rid of the negative words and replace them with the Word of God. Have you ever just listened to the conversations that you have with others? A lot can be said about who you are by the conversations that you keep. You can always tell when someone spends time with the Lord because the conversations have the Lord all through them. While I was in the process of being healed, I had to be very careful about whom I allowed around me and what conversations I entertained. My healing and peace were dependent on it.

Take a few minutes...

and write down the names of your close acquaintances. Below I have two sections. One section is for your closest friends and the other section is for you. Write a note about your conversations with them. Are they mostly positive or are they negative? Are they draining or uplifting? There is a lot to be said about who you are and whom you allow around you by the conversations you keep. Are these friends drawing you closer to Jesus or further away?

Name your closest friends:

1._____

2._____

3._____

4._____

5._____

Types of Conversations: Positive or Negative?

1. _____

_____

_____

_____

2. _____

_____

_____

_____

3. _____

_____

_____

_____

4. _____

_____

_____

_____

5. _____

_____

_____

_____

Day 5

I had not been to church now for two Sundays, and it felt unusual. What was I going to do all day? Well, I watched the Word Network and waited until after the 8 o'clock service to request a copy of the DVD. I called Larry, a deacon at our church, and asked him to send someone by with the DVD from the 8 o'clock service. He laughed and said, "I knew you were going to call." He said he would give a copy to my best friend and have her drop it off to me.

It is now 10:30 a.m., and "The Warden" went to the store to get something; I don't even remember what. No one is here but me, and there is a knock at the door. My best friend is standing outside, waiting for me to open the door. She said she could not stay because I had to rest. I asked her to come in and sit down for a while, but she declined. I informed her that "The Warden" went to the store, and no one was here with me. I could sense that something was wrong even though she was smiling. When you pull away to be with Jesus, you become more sensitive to things around you, good or bad. I coerced her to come in, and I asked her what was wrong? She began to share about an unhealthy relationship her daughter was in. It was a relationship that she did not approve of. As we were discussing it, I could feel the pain and confusion that was going on in her heart.

    My best friend was struggling with her love for her daughter and walking in obedience to God's word. She was trying to find wisdom on how to support her daughter without compromising the Word of God. She reminded me of Jesus when she decided to tell her daughter, though I don't support your decision, you are still my child, and I love you. Jesus does that with us, His children, all the time. He continually forgives us when we repent and continues to show love even when we are wrong. Through Christ's example of walking in love, we can follow His standards and allow love to lead in every struggle and every disagreement. When we do, love will always leave an open door to healing and restoration.

Jesus doesn't always like the decisions that we make, but He never stops loving us. His love for us always draws us back into His presence again. I believe that disobedience has its consequences, and we will pay for those consequences eventually if we don't change. My prayer for her daughter is that repentance comes quickly so that the consequences do not have to be as severe.

It is now 11:15 a.m. I know that church services have already started. My assistant came back from the store, and when she saw my best friend, the first thing she said was, "I hope you're not dumping on Pastor Gwen because she needs her rest." My best friend is so funny! She jumped up like a three-year-old and ran to the door like a child caught stealing out of a candy jar! My best friend kissed me on my cheek and scurried to the door. The Warden gave her a look! You know that look as if she was going to get spanked. So, she left. The rest of the day, I did absolutely nothing but rest.

As I thought about my best friend and her daughter's situation, I started reminiscing about times when I was disobedient yet still felt God's love. The enemy will try to make you think that when you disobey the Word of God or when you sin against God, that He's mad at you or that He's done with you. That is such a lie! Jesus says that He will never leave you nor forsake you. He will be with you always, even until the end of the world. I believe He will. Do you?

Journal Your Thoughts

I have suffered the consequences of my wrong decisions many times, and like the prodigal son, I went off and did my thing my way, but when I came to myself, love was always waiting for me to return.

Can you still feel the love of God in you or around you? Love is not just a feeling; it is also confidence in what you know. Where are you in your life right now concerning your relationship with Jesus? Are you walking as closely as you used to? Use the lines below and journal where you are with your walk with your Savior. Do you know that He loves you even in times of disobedience?

_____

_____

_____

_____

_____

_____

_____

_____

Day 6

Day six, and it is 5:50 a.m. I felt in my spirit to pray for a friend of mine named Michelle. She is a member of our church. I had a dream that she was not feeling well, and I decided to call her and check on her even though I was told, no ministry. I tried to call her several times, but there was no answer. I wish I could talk to her as I had visions of her in the hospital and on bed rest. I felt the spirit telling me to just pray for her. I wanted to talk to her, but the Spirit of the Lord said that all I needed to do was pray.

He said, "You don't have to talk to people every time I place them on your heart." He reminded me that my prayers are just as effective, if not more effective, than a phone call, and our prayers can reach further than our conversations any day.

Prayer is powerful. It can transcend time and space and can reach an eternal Heaven that is always open for God's children. More than anyone's presence, you need their prayers. Why? Because while I am physically trying to reach you, prayer can get to heaven instantly. God said in His Word, "Men ought to always pray." So, in obedience to the Word, I prayed. I believe Michelle is all the better because I did. Jesus also said, "Father, I know you hear me; you always hear me." If we believe that Jesus said, then when we pray, we should be confident that our prayers are heard and answered. I continued praying, being led by the Holy Spirit; I noticed, the more I prayed, the more I wanted to pray.

When I give myself over to prayer, the Holy Spirit takes the lead and gently guides me to the destination where I can hear Him clearly. In that prayer time, the Spirit of God infused my thoughts and told me to start writing about my journey to recovery. He instructed me to write this journal. The idea of me writing this journal became a bit overwhelming as I thought about how many pages it would be and how I can write a journal when I am not an author.

I sat in silence, trying to process the negative thoughts that had infiltrated my mind, repeatedly saying, "I can't do it." As the enemy lies about my ability to write this journal, the fight begins, "You can't write a journal." He flooded my mind with negative thoughts and excuses as to why I couldn't do it! I prayed and heard the Holy Spirit whisper and say, "You can do all things through Me who strengthens you."

Peace, serenity, and confidence began to overtake me like crashing waves hitting the shore of my soul. "And yes, I can, and I will write this journal."

Journal Your Thoughts

Can you see the importance of prayer? What has the enemy lied to you about and stopped you from doing because you did not pray? Did you lack faith? What you are sensing, hearing, or feeling as you wait patiently in His presence in prayer.

_____
_____
_____
_____
_____
_____
_____
_____
_____
_____
_____
_____
_____
_____
_____
_____

An Experience

I want to share an experience I had with the Lord while praying, which confirmed that I would write this journal and many others books. The Bible says, "As a man thinks in his heart, so is he." I said, "Abba, if you want me to be an author, then confirm it. That is precisely what He did that day.

My family came home after 5 p.m. I took a break to watch a movie with them called "The Kiss." The film was about a writer who had written a book twenty years prior and did not finish it. He had submitted the book unfinished to his publishing company, and a young editor found the book and fell in love with it. In the film, she searched to find the author so that she could get him to write the rest of the book. The young lady found the author and inspired him to finish the book. Ironic, huh?

God uses anything around us to confirm what it is He is calling us to do. I have many books in my spirit that need to be written, but I never sit down long enough to write them.

Now, I must be still because of this pneumonia, and I also have time to write. I believe God allowed me to watch that movie to encourage me to finish the books that are inside of me.

I feel like this journey right now is truly ordained by God. The movies, visitors, the visitations of the Spirit, the phone calls, and even the babysitting, done by my assistant, everything that I was experiencing right now had a purpose. Pray with me as you are reading this journal.

My Prayer

God, I know that you are going to reveal every purpose as I continue this journey of fourteen days with You. I feel closer to You, Father, more than I ever have. I feel so vital to You. I feel so loved by You. Most of all, I'm glad you're jealous for me. I am growing in my jealousy for You and our time together. I pray for the one who is reading this book. I am asking that You would touch them right now in their spirit, Father and allow them to feel Your presence of peace and love. In Jesus' name, Amen.

How Do You Feel at This Very Moment?

How do you feel since you have been on this journey? Can you feel yourself drawing closer to the Lord? Can you feel His love and His peace? Take this moment to journal and talk about how you feel right now.

_____
_____
_____
_____
_____
_____
_____
_____
_____
_____
_____
_____
_____
_____
_____
_____
_____

Day 7

Today was a day of deep reflection. I didn't do much but think and reflect on how I got so far away from peace. Though I have been experiencing physical illness, I could not help but think of all of the mental battles that I experienced when this recovery began. Father, thank You for this peace and quiet. I am writing by the Holy Spirit's leading on this beautiful day, and I can get used to this sweet peace! Why are we so afraid of peace? Are we fearful that you will tell us something we don't want to hear if we're sitting in silence? Are we afraid of peace because we are so indoctrinated with confusion that peace is a threat to our sanity? When did peace become our enemy? Maybe we are afraid to sit in peace because we know we need to reconcile things we would rather forget...hmm. That is a stop and think about it moment right there. Maybe, we know that our God is waiting to sit and talk with us, and for some strange reason, we just don't want to hear it.

When did I become afraid of the

presence of God? The Bible says that in His presence is the fullness of joy, and at His right hand, there are pleasures forevermore. I know the Word of God is true, and yet, there is warfare continuously in our souls when we do not sit and deal with our unresolved issues. I would love to blame all of this on the enemy of my soul, who is constantly bringing distractions to keep me from reading the Word of God, but it's me who allows it. The Bible says, "In the beginning was the Word and the Word was with God and the Word was God." So, when we sit down to read the Word of God, we are sitting with Jesus as the living Word.

    Do you know what is odd? It's challenging to get into the presence of God when so many distractions surround us but, when we get there, we don't want to leave. The American dream is real, but we work so much chasing that dream that we almost have to restrain ourselves to sit and be still. When we do discipline ourselves enough to sit, our minds are distracted and begin to wander. We think about all the things we need to do or should have done. Our thoughts are continually processing information, much like a computer. Social media has not made this any easier. We've grown addicted to our gadgets, and even our children find it impossible to be away from their phones or tablets. What a shame. Do you find it difficult to just sit with a book or be in total silence?

Computers need defragmentation to get rid of the things that slow their processing down. As children of God, we should take time to defrag so that we don't slow down God's processes in our lives.

I am on day seven. Help me, Lord! How long have I been running like this? How long have I been striving in this fashion? Father, I thank you for sustaining me. I realize now that I have been moving this way for far too long. Father, it is only You that has kept me alive for this long. I wonder, who else has been running like this? I won't even try to put a number on it. I'll only speak for myself, but I will challenge you with the same questions. How long have you been running?

I want to share a personal memory with you about something my Godfather, James Scott, said to me. He passed away almost ten years ago, but before he died, he told me, "Slow down, baby. You're moving too fast." There was something about the way he said it that made me stop and look at him.

He looked at me with dimming eyes as death was carefully creeping upon him. I saw a glimmer of life come back long enough to get my attention. He repeated it, "Baby girl. Slow down." I told him I would slow down, but I never did until the time came where I had to. It was NOT because I wanted to. What is the hurry? I was running at an unnatural pace. Was I afraid that I was not going to fulfill my destiny? Did I feel like I was behind where I was supposed to be at this age? What was driving me to run so fast, fight so hard, and push so relentlessly! Where did that come from? Did I think I was going to miss something?

Why do we put so much pressure on the destination that we forget the joy in the journey?

I want you to pray this simple prayer.

Father, I love You so much, and I want You to be proud of me. I realize that what I am in pursuit of is what I already have. Father, I know that You are so proud of us already, and why wouldn't You be? We are Your creation. The Bible says in Jeremiah 29:11, "Your thoughts toward us are good and not evil to give us hope and a future." You placed the responsibility upon Yourself to give us hope and a future. So, Father, I submit to Your desire, and I surrender to Your future for me. No, more striving beyond my limits. There will be no more pushing beyond the boundaries that are set around me to protect me. I am not going to miss my purpose or my destiny. I am not going to miss one thing.

I rest in the presence of God for my life, for real. Your Word declares, "You that began a good work are well able to perform it." So, let the performance begin. It is showtime in my life, and the author of the script is my Savior. Jesus, You wrote the script, and You are directing it. You are producing it, and You are the lead role in it. What is my part in the production? I am co-starring! Yay, Jesus! The significant part about doing Your script Father is that the only thing I must do is to show up and do my part. My one part. That's it! I don't have to do dual roles. Father, I thank You! – Amen!

After Reading Day Seven

Share your thoughts with me. Are you pushing yourself too hard? Are you having trouble sleeping? What are you striving to do, and who is pressuring you? Take time to journal the journey, and as you reflect on the journey, stop, and celebrate the victories.

_____
_____
_____
_____
_____
_____
_____
_____
_____
_____
_____
_____
_____
_____
_____
_____
_____
_____

Day 8

Today is a day of prayer. While I was sitting here searching on my iPad, I believe the Holy Spirit led me to research material from Morris Cerullo Ministries. I came across a book called "Teach Me How to Pray" This book is life-giving and insightful. Things are coming together now, at least in my spirit.

It is still early, around 9 a.m. or so. I am sitting here listening to music while I am praying. A song comes on about prayer. Ironically, I would be listening to the song while reading this book, wouldn't you say? I love these God moments. I feel and know in my spirit that God is at work, and I am excited. There is about to be a visitation, and I know it. While sitting there, I see myself climbing up a mountain, and the Lord is guiding me upward. In this vision, there are some places that I can't reach on my own, and I see the hand of the Lord reaching down to help me up when I need it. He is pulling me upward as always. My spirit is driving me, and I'm excited to be on this journey with my Father.

It is now 10:49 a.m., and I am interrupted by the doorbell. I rise to answer it. Willetra, Tasha, and Naomi are here to clean my house two days before Thanksgiving. This cleaning is so much more significant than Thanksgiving in my spirit. Out with the old and in with the new. Oh my God! The rushing energy in my spirit right now is tangible. Father, I know when You are up to something. Everything that's going on around me is significant to the change that's happening in me.

I am so excited to have more adult company around me, and my spirit is so ready to pour out to them. As I am talking to them, I feel the presence of the Lord, and there are so many things that I want to say to them. I want to share with them the importance of spending time with the Lord. I want to share the importance of prayer, but this is not yet the time.

I must stop myself much like a jockey pulling the reins of a champion horse who is anxious to sprint through the gates at full speed. I am ready to give out every revelation, epiphany, and insight given to me by the Father. However, it is not time to share everything. The Holy Spirit said, "Not yet." I don't know the fullness of what the Father is doing in me, but I know that the time of pouring has not yet come.

Journal Your Thoughts

Can you feel the moving of the Holy Spirit as you read this chapter? Take a moment and journal. What are you feeling? What do you believe He is saying to you? Don't overthink it. Write what you are feeling or sensing at this very moment.

_____
_____
_____
_____
_____
_____
_____
_____
_____
_____
_____
_____
_____
_____
_____
_____

Day 9

Today is the day before Thanksgiving, and I am so excited that Chauncey is home from New York. Yay, Jesus! It feels like my children are the only connection with the outside world right now since the ladies cleaned my house yesterday. I know that sounds dramatic. It was only yesterday. I feel life flowing through me, and I am getting stronger every day, about 85% better now. I am sitting alone for a moment and hear my spirit saying, "Father, You are always in the shadows of my mind and heart. My existence is in You." Father, Your Word says, "Where can I go from your presence?" I don't ever want to leave your presence again; this is real peace.

It is about 8 p.m. now, and here he is, Chauncey is here! Yay! Jason, my oldest son, has also come over, and all my children are home. Thank you, Father, for the gift of family. We all hugged and settled in the house. I began to sing, and everyone joined in. Our harmonies blend with the sound of unity; this must be what the angels in Heaven sound like when they worship. Our harmonies ring throughout the house, and you hear nothing but love. When we sing, there is no attention-seeking, no competition for sound or solo just wonders coming from every heart filled with all colors of love. My husband, Charlie, is leading this song now, and we all join in with smiles and giggles because Charlie always sings loud and really hard! I don't even remember what the name of the song was. We just sang and laughed.

The older I become, the more important family is illuminated in my mind. I believe the Father is pleased as families come together in love. I think about all the time I spend with others and how out of balance my priorities are. I unknowingly neglect my own family. Not good!

Are you spending quality time with your family? Ask the Lord if you are neglecting them, adjust, and apologies if necessary. I can now see God's love through His gift of family. What love the Father has for us!

No tangible instrument, no logical deductions by the wisest of men, no ocean deep, and no eternity long enough can measure the love of the Father in its epic proportions. The love of the Father transcends time and space and encompasses everything. It is more than the air we breathe. It is more powerful than death. The Bible says, "Where can I go from His presence?" The answer is nowhere. The Father's love for us is unfathomable, unbreakable, and everlasting. Wow, I feel God's presence right now. "Can it get any better than this?"

Experiencing God's Love

There are many ways we can experience God's love. Below are some pages that I want you to use to express how you have experienced His love. Take a moment, and then start journaling. It can be through family, friends, or nature. Let the Holy Spirit recall the ways you have experienced His love.

_____
_____
_____
_____
_____
_____
_____
_____
_____
_____
_____
_____
_____
_____
_____
_____
_____
_____

Let's Continue the Story

Thanksgiving Dinner started around 5 p.m. My aunt Nell came early and brought some shrimp. I love shrimp and crackers. My mom and dad came next. We fixed Granny a plate and had my daughter, Victoria, take it to her house. This Thanksgiving was the first Thanksgiving without Granny being there because she had a cold and stayed home. Granny is now 86 years old, and I'm so thankful to God that she's still alive.

The company of friends and family started trailing in for our traditional game of Taboo. It usually begins around 7:30 p.m. We have played this high-energy game for several years now, at least the last seven or so. Laughter and love filled the house, and the atmosphere was chaotic and explosive. I love this game and the people that stayed to play. I have been up for 12 hours now, and I can feel my strength leaving me. I've learned to listen to my body, so I fixed myself a nice cup of hot tea and drifted silently downstairs, hoping no one noticed, so they could continue having fun.

As I descended downstairs like a thief on the prowl, looking around carefully so no one would see, I hear the loud voices that filled my home. The voices became quieter and quieter as my focus shifted from them to me, my rest, my peace, my sanctuary, and my soft, warm, inviting bed.

Ah! What a perfect ending to a wonderful day; thank you, Jesus! As I pondered the day, I am so thankful to my 18-year-old daughter, Victoria, who stayed up almost 24 hours cooking and preparing for this incredible day. Not only is she wise and beautiful, but she can cook. Everything that she made smelled mouthwatering and tasted delicious. She took over cooking, and I appreciate her for it. She knows that Thanksgiving is my absolute favorite holiday, and she made sure that I had my day and enjoyed it.

What Do You Feel?

Do you feel the subtle wooing of the Spirit pulling on you to come and spend some time with Him? Do you feel an unction to pray? Take a moment and write a heartfelt prayer of thanks for family and friends.

_____
_____
_____
_____
_____
_____
_____
_____
_____
_____
_____
_____
_____
_____
_____
_____

Day 10

Today, I slept until 12:45 p.m. and felt as if I could sleep some more but, I hear the sweet voice of my mom upstairs, making her way gracefully down to my room. We began to reminisce about last night, and she told me how much she and my dad enjoyed themselves with all the family and friends on this Thanksgiving Day. She said she was glad I was still in bed. She told me to take my time moving around because my resistance was still low. She kissed me in her gentle, loving way and left.

My mother is one of the most loving people I know. I grew up watching my mother take care of the neighborhood. None of my friends knew her real name. Everyone just called her mom. I believe her ministry is to transition people from this life to eternal life because while growing up, my mom took care of people in our apartment complex that was terminally ill. God seems always to place my mother somewhere where someone needed her. I laugh because she tells me that I need to slow down and not allow people to pull on me so much, but that is what she did. I think my ministry is an extension of hers. She is my Elijah!

I have a godson named Adam, and he called to check on me. We began a wonderful conversation about the scriptures. We talked about Elijah, Elisha, and Gehazi. I would subtopic our conversation, *Motive, Mantle, and Relationship.* The Spirit of wisdom was hovering in our conversation, and I knew the Lord was with us. I have become more sensitive to the Holy Spirit since being in the house these fourteen days.

We talked about Elisha and how he served Elijah. We talked about how Elisha stayed with his mentor up until the time that his mentor was taken away by God in a whirlwind. One of the problems with young ministers in ministry is that everyone wants a title, but no one wants the process. I wouldn't say I like the process, but I submit to the process anyway because we gain wisdom, strength, maturity, and realize the necessity of obedience.

The revelation God gave me concerning Elijah and Elisha is that Elisha was committed to serving Elijah. Elisha had been trained by the best and did not allow his ambition to override his obedience. The relationship between Elijah and Elisha was so intimate that Elisha called Elijah father. God establishes divine mentorship. The mentor knows his assignment, and the mentee knows his placement.

Elisha kept his eyes on his mentor until the day the Lord took Elijah home. The relationship between Elisha and Gehazi was very different. Although externally, it looked the same. The heart of Gehazi was very different from that of Elisha's. If you read the story in the Bible, Gehazi wanted to be an Elisha. Gehazi thought that he deserved something for serving the great man of God.

In 2 Kings, chapter 5, you will see that Elijah was offered money and clothing for healing an official who had heard about the healing miracles at the hand of Elisha. But Elisha declined. Elisha said it was not time to take any money or clothing offered by the now healed official. Elisha's obedience to God would not allow him to take anything from the official. When the official left, Gehazi went after him and said Elisha changed his mind and wanted the money and the clothing. Gehazi took the clothing and money and hid them in his tent. Elisha later sent for Gehazi and asked him, "Where have you gone?" Gehazi lied and replied, "I have not gone anywhere." Elijah, the prophet, asks, "Did not my spirit go with you when you went to the official and got the money and clothing?" Now the character of Gehazi was exposed!

It is crucial that we practice introspection. When we introspect, we allow God to show us the areas in our character that need to be developed. He will show us our weaknesses so that we would come to Him for help. We always need the sifting of the Holy Ghost to reveal areas where we struggle in our character. We need Him to show us the areas that could bring reproach upon the Name of the Lord and His church. We need Him to show us these areas of struggle in our character or generational curses that come through our family line. Only the Holy Spirit can show us these things. Many times, He uses our mentors to help us mature in our areas of struggle.

Here we are talking about mentors again. It is essential to have a mentor. A mentor helps guide you through life's journey and helps us make Godly decisions in a world with so much temptation. We sometimes, like Gehazi, will trade time with God with fleshly desires; I know because I have done it a few times. A mentor will pray for you and remind you who you are and how important it is to spend quality time with God and allow Him in prayer to show you, YOU!

Do you have someone in your life with a Godly character who loves you and will speak the truth to you, even when it hurts? Someone who will hold you accountable when you are drifting from the presence of the Lord?

Who Are They?
Name them One by One.

Write their names down below and then call them and thank them for holding you accountable. Spend some time praying for them and thanking God for allowing them to be in your life.

_____
_____
_____
_____
_____
_____
_____
_____
_____
_____
_____
_____
_____
_____
_____
_____
_____
_____

Day 11

Day eleven was very calm and relaxing. My son, Chauncey, and I are watching television and talking about his spiritual life. He is attending Berklee School of Music in Boston. We talked about the necessity of him finding a church home, and I explained that if we feed our carnal man more than we feed our spiritual man, our spiritual man will become weak and find ourselves doing things that we never thought we would do. I explained the importance of having the Word of God around him. I reminded him that it is by the grace of God that he is even in that college.

How much time are you spending in the Word of God? Do you have a church home? When was the last time you just sat reading the Word of God? When was the last time you prayed? We can have so many excuses for not going to church, but the Word of God says we should not get into the bad habit of not going. Read Hebrews 10:25. Not going is disobedience to God. I want you to write down why you stopped going and then measure those excuses by God's Word and repent. Repentance means changing directions, attitudes, and behavior.

Journal Your Thoughts

Have you stopped going to church? If so, why did you stop going?

_____
_____
_____
_____
_____
_____
_____
_____
_____
_____
_____
_____
_____
_____
_____
_____
_____
_____
_____
_____

Day 12

Today is day twelve, and my husband's alarm awakens me around 5 a.m. I am praying for my healing and my son, Chauncey. I prayed that the Lord would fill him up again with His Holy Spirit. I prayed for the church and for all of the people that will be visiting church today. Today is Sunday, and I was home and still recovering, so I prayed that my husband would sustain the anointing and yield himself to the leading of the Holy Spirit as he ran the Church service in my absence.

I made my way upstairs into the living room. There I was, sitting quietly in my favorite spot. I was reminded of God's love yet again and knew I needed to get into the Word of God. I reached for the iPad and began to read John 1:35 to the end of the chapter. In John 1:35, John the Baptist stood with two other disciples. John said, "Behold the Lamb of God." When the disciples heard John say this, they turned and followed Jesus. We must make sure we always follow Jesus, and our love for Him should guide us to His presence.

I do remember, as I started working in ministry, that I stopped taking walks with God. Imagine your employer calling meetings and you being too preoccupied to attend them. What happens if your employer changes existing policies or changes the direction of the team in those meetings? You are misaligned because you have missed those meetings, and you begin to make mistakes; this is what my busy season felt like for me. I had forgotten that Jesus was my employer. I was missing important meetings with Him. I began to run the church based on my intellect. I began to run my life from my desires. Oh, I wish you could hear me sighing right now. I got burnt out and frustrated. Things started happening around me that I did not know how to handle.

Take a moment and breathe in this Revelation. Take a moment, and ask yourself, is this you too? Verse 38 of the same chapter says that Jesus turned and saw them following Him and said to them, "What do you seek?" "What do you want? "Why are you following me?" (This part is difficult for me to share, but here it goes!) I had to question my motives as to why I was following Jesus. I remember, at first, it was out of love and adoration. It was a desire to be a child of God who loves her Father.

I was excited about working for God and ministry! I started with the right intentions and the right heart but, when the people came and the ministry's demands became more demanding, I stopped talking to the Lord as much, or at least until I needed His help with a situation. My prayer time got shorter as I got busier.

I hate to admit this, but here it goes, uugghh! I am struggling to say this. As I got busier, I felt the people's demands, and I also felt self-important, which made me self-reliant. There I said it. How embarrassing. But true. The more the people needed me, the more important I felt.

Have you had a moment like this? What did it look like for you? I had to go back to the beginning. I had to go back to why I was following Jesus. I had to look in the mirror and ask myself, "Am I exchanging my passion for Jesus for my passion for the people?". These character checks are essential as we rise in any occupation. I had to see what I had become. I asked myself, "What am I doing, and why am I doing it?" Was I lacking something that was being validated by the people, and that made me feel important and noticed? Jesus already sees me as perfect, and I know this, but I could not see myself as perfect. We have to be careful that we are not seeking validation from people who did not create us and receive what God says about us, the one that created us.

I decided on the couch to get back to that place or move forward from this one. I have decided to show up at the meetings with the Lord, my employer, in prayer. I have decided to show up whether He speaks or not because I love Him and love being with Him in prayer.

Jesus lovingly began to talk to me about my motives and why I do the things I do. I do some things because I am concerned about God's people, but that can never override what God says to do. Sometimes I do things because it is fun or exciting, and I forget to check in with God before committing to things. I forgot to talk to the maker of all things. Sometimes I did things to appease the people because I'm not too fond of confrontation.

I had to start praying for God to check my character and my motives for doing anything anymore. In John 1:38, Jesus asked the disciples what they wanted? When people join your ministry or your organization of any kind, ask them what they want. If God told them to follow, He would say to them, "why?". If they do not know, ask them to go pray, and when they have an answer, come back and tell you. People must understand why they are following the God in you, and you must know why they are following you. People have all kinds of motives as to why they wish to follow you.

Some follow because they know they need something and will position themselves as students.
Some think they are your teacher and won't stay very long because the shepherd will never be a student to the sheep. Some come because they are looking for a position or title. People like that will only stay around or work if they

get one. These people typically battle with low self-esteem and need to be validated by someone other than Jesus. They want to walk close to you or get close to people in power trying to gain favor by association. Some people flatter leadership or pastors, even going as far as buying them expensive items to gain favor or to gain a position. Some people want to be a part of the next new growing church to keep up with the so-called church *Joneses*. (I made that one up).

People like that have no root system and will love you when you are new and exciting and discredit you and leave if they don't get what they want. Some people come into a church by association; they know that you know people they consider powerful or generals in the faith, and they want to hang close enough to be seen with you. People like that think if they stay close enough to you, other people in leadership will believe they are anointed too, by association. They also think that by staying close enough and saying the right things in others' presence, someone will hear them and open a platform for them to speak on. Others are looking for you to fill a void in their lives, so you can become their parent, such as a mother, aunt, or mentor, anything to position themselves in a close relationship that they believe will bring them opportunities that should only be given over time.

The problem with this type of behavior is that if the person has bad relationships with these different family members or work affiliates, they will eventually have a problem with you and treat you with the same disrespect they do with their family members. I have had to deal with this type of behavior, and dealing with it without prayer and patience can be overwhelming. It is so detrimental to have quiet time in prayer with the Lord when dealing with people. We have to keep our eyes fixed on Jesus, the Author, and Finisher of our faith.

Journal Your Thoughts

Have you had to deal with people on your job or in the church that were challenging? What have you learned this day that you will apply to these situations? Journal below and share your thoughts.

_____
_____
_____
_____
_____
_____
_____
_____
_____
_____
_____
_____
_____
_____
_____
_____

Day 13

Here I am at my favorite spot again, my couch upstairs in the living room! I got up early to meet with the Lord and began to pray. There is a song that says, "Tis so sweet to trust in Jesus, just to take Him at His Word." What a sweet time of fellowship. I realize that I have allowed so many things to pull me out of my time with the Lord. I can now see how out of balance I had become. I see how far I have gone, and I began to weep. Father, forgive me! I pray that you will remove all the spiritual calluses off my heart and cleanse me. I am reminded of the love relationship that the Lord and I have and where my strength has been coming from and I am humbled - humbled because His love did not allow me to destroy myself. He has been carrying me this whole time. What a great God You are?

My son, Chauncey, is going back to Boston, and I am helping him pack. I had the absolute pleasure of staying up late last night spending time with both my sons. We were on the couch together, holding hands and loving each other as if every moment were the last. My boys are men now and have their own lives. I know that I taught them everything I could and have to trust that what I've placed in their spirits about the Lord will remain. I am reflecting on this because it is so important that we spend quality time with our children just as we spend quality time with our Lord. Our children are gifts from God, and He expects us to take time to care for them spiritually as well as naturally.

Our focus on work and ministry, if we are not careful, can overwhelm our lives. We can easily push our families behind the church and our careers, and God is not pleased with that. When we do that, our families feel that they have to compete with our ministry or career, which is out of God's order. God ordained family before He ordained the church. We must be faithful parents and spouses so that the enemy cannot get a foothold in our lives or our families. We don't want to cause any unnecessary warfare in our homes. We must pray and seek the Lord concerning any character issues that may drive our souls away from the presence of the Lord. We need to pray that we are led by the Spirit of God and not our selfish desires. We also must walk honestly with ourselves and with God so we do not make excuses for negative behaviors and struggles. We must constantly seek the Lord in prayer and not just for others but for ourselves also. We must desire truth in our inward parts, at the very core of who we are. We need to be naked and vulnerable before the Lord.

We should pray as David did in Psalms 139, "Search me oh Lord and know my heart, try me and know my anxious thoughts and if you see any wicked thing in me, take it out and lead me in your everlasting way." When we do this and take the time to listen, God, Himself will speak and share those intricate things we need to hear; whether we like it or not, it is good for us because Jesus does all things well.

Journal Your Thoughts

Let's stop and journal right now. What thoughts are coming to you as you read this day? Are you thinking about a quiet time with the Lord? Do you think about family? What are you feeling?

_____
_____
_____
_____
_____
_____
_____
_____
_____
_____
_____
_____
_____
_____
_____
_____
_____

Day 14

Day fourteen! You made it. Today is the last day and the first day. Why the last day? I went to the doctor's office to do a follow-up, and the doctor Dr. Kurisu said my lungs were clear. He said I can go out of the house now, but to take it slow. I told him that I am still fatigued after moving around a bit. He said that it is normal after pneumonia. My doctor said to me again, "Take it slow!" I heard my doctor, but I also heard the Holy Spirit whisper and tell me to take it slow as well. I know that it is important for me to slow down, not just my body but also my mind. I have to remember that my priority is to continually spend time with the Lord, now and for the rest of my life. I understand that spending time away from the church and away from people is good for me and good for the congregation. When I am healthy, my family and the church are healthy too.

I call it the first day because I have started my life over again with the Lord. I have an excitement in my spirit that I have not felt in a long time. I will be spending more time in prayer, worship, and fellowship with the Lord. I have unplugged from the matrix, and I swallowed the red pill. If you have never seen "The Matrix," watch the movie, and you will get the analogy. What I am trying to say is, I can see clearly again. My life will never be the same. These fourteen days of reflection have brought me correction, insight, repentance, revelation, deliverance, and healing.

    I pray in the name of Jesus that you feel the Spirit of God, calling you back into that intimate place with Him again. I pray you find many places where you can be alone with the Lord to love on Him and appreciate Him as the son of God but also your Father, and He's a good Father. I pray that we do not get so busy doing the work that we forget the employer. I pray that your fire begins to burn again with the white fire that purifies our hearts continually. I pray for every Pastor who is overwhelmed and overworked. I pray that you will take the time to unplug and get away to spend time alone with the lover of your soul,

Jesus! I pray that every young minister seeking the great platform will cancel that agenda and desire to please the Lord day by day. You have already received the highest honor there is, and that is being a child of God! I pray for every new believer. Never give up on Jesus because He will never give up on you. We will make mistakes all along this walk towards perfection, but God's grace and His love for us will always lead us back to His presence again and again. I pray this journal will escort you back to the feet of the One True and Living God, in Jesus's name. Amen!

The Beginning!

www.ingramcontent.com/pod-product-compliance
Lightning Source LLC
Chambersburg PA
CBHW071404290426
44108CB00014B/1681